*1 - The Hands and Feet of Christ*

# THE HANDS AND FEET OF CHRIST

# THE HANDS AND FEET OF CHRIST

## Nine Models for Eucharistic Ministers

### STANLEY   KONIECZNY

ALBA · HOUSE  NEW · YORK

SOCIETY OF ST. PAUL, 2187 VICTORY BLVD., STATEN ISLAND, NEW YORK 10314

*ISBN 0-8189-0515-8*

*Designed, printed and bound in the United States of
America by the Fathers and Brothers of the
Society of St. Paul, 2187 Victory Boulevard,
Staten Island, New York 10314, as part of their
communications apostolate.*

*1 2 3 4 5 6 7 8 9 (Current Printing: first digit)*

The material in this pamphlet
first appeared in serial form in
*Eucharistic Minister*, published by
Celebration Publications, Kansas
City, MO 64141.

*Illustrations by artist*
Joe Roy

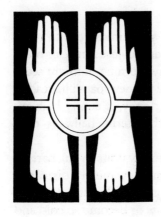

# Introduction

*"Christ has no body now*
*on earth, but yours;*
*No hands but yours;*
*No feet but yours."*

ST. TERESA OF AVILA

T HE CALL to serve as a Eucharistic minister for the sick and shut-ins can open the door to one of the most rewarding apostolates in the Church today. In this special ministry, thousands of men and women from all walks of life have found opportunities to become the hands and feet of Jesus Christ. By bringing the Blessed Sacrament to those who suffer from illness, isolation and the effects of old age, Eucharistic ministers can enter into a very intimate relationship with both Jesus and the infirmed people whom they serve.

Without a doubt, this ministry can be a rich opportunity for growth. Yet, there is always the human element of such outreach which can fall short of the ideal. Eucharistic ministers can either "burn-out" or end up just going through the motions. When they lose sight of the beauty and wealth of this service, they can re-charge their enthusiasm and zest in the great heritage upon which their apostolate is grounded.

The following meditations are geared to heighten the awareness of the great tradition in which Eucharistic ministers operate. Many heroic men and women throughout the history of the Church have been called to be the hands and the feet of

Christ. Today's Eucharistic ministers sometimes need to recall those who in the past have bravely carried Jesus into an often hostile world. On a cold, damp Sunday morning, it might seem more sensible to stay at home and read the newspaper instead of tramping about visiting shut-ins. Certainly, a sunny ballpark appears much more inviting than the sterile hallways of a convalescent center.

On the other hand, weekly or monthly visits by Eucharistic ministers can become so routine that they merely distribute hosts instead of sharing the Body of Christ. Eucharistic ministers could either dread their appointed visits or become so cold and impersonal that their ministry is mechanical.

There comes a time in either instance when Eucharistic ministers might question their worth and purpose. At times like these, they might want to remember Who they serve and who served before them. Hopefully, this booklet will bring them a sense of the heroic generosity and creativity exhibited by those who served in previous times. For those who have never doubted or dreaded their calling, these chapters can lend themselves to moments of reflection and remembrance; healthy acts for anyone who serves.

The following meditations are rooted both in the past and in the present. The incidents from the lives of nine saintly women and men are linked with parallel experiences of contemporary Eucharistic ministers to the sick and shut-in. These modern-day instances touch on some of the universal concerns of Eucharistic ministers as they serve people who confront terminal illness, the deterioration of aging and the terrible poverty of loneliness which all too often accompanies sickness and old age.

The example of these men and women, the former hands and feet of Christ, can stir the faith and charity of today's Eucharistic ministers who will assist Jesus as He dispels the fear and loneliness of sickness and death from our fellow Catholics confined to their homes, hospitals and nursing centers.

# Nine Models for
# Eucharistic Ministers

# I

# *The Church Of The Home*

THE NEW TESTAMENT offers only brief glimpses of the ministry of Sts. Aquila and Priscilla. The apostolate of these friends of St. Paul closely parallels the work of many husband-and-wife teams of Eucharistic ministers who reach out to today's infirmed and elderly.

Sts. Aquila and Priscilla were exiled Jewish tentmakers, living in Corinth after being driven from Rome during Emperor Claudius' persecution. The Acts of the Apostles notes that St. Paul made his home with this couple when he visited Corinth. In fact, they might have been his first converts in this ancient Greek port. The relationship of Sts. Aquila and Priscilla and the Apostle to the Gentiles blossomed to the point where St. Paul would later refer to them as "fellow workers in the service of Christ."

From these Scriptural references, the twofold apostolate of Sts. Aquila and Priscilla emerges. They were ministers of the

Word and of the Eucharist. Their teaching ministry is evident at Ephesus where they instructed Apollos, the Alexandrian, in the Good News. As Eucharistic ministers, this couple opened their very home as a meeting place of the Christian community. The Lord's Supper was celebrated in their home. The hospitality and generosity of Sts. Aquila and Priscilla provided home churches in both Corinth and Rome.

Yet, none of this was accomplished without a cost. In his letter to the Romans, St. Paul noted that his friends, Aquila and Priscilla, had jeopardized their own lives for the sake of the Gospel and for St. Paul himself. Today, the Church honors Sts. Aquila and Priscilla as martyrs for the faith although it is disputed whether the couple made their ultimate sacrifice for Christ in Rome or Asia Minor.

‡　　‡　　‡

THE WIVES AND HUSBANDS who serve together as Eucharistic ministers can find special inspiration in the lives of Sts. Aquila and Priscilla. The love and faith at the bedrock of married life can be especially supportive to husband-and-wife Eucharistic ministers as they strive to be open and take risks like these special friends of St. Paul.

Sts. Aquila and Priscilla established the Church in their own home. Their example calls for a certain selfless hospitality and openness. Contemporary Eucharistic ministers bring their parishes to the homes and sickrooms of their patients. Warmth and friendliness should be the hallmarks of these modern home-churches.

Eucharistic ministers need to be aware that for the infirmed and shut-ins, they represent the entire parish family. These parish visitors should allow a few minutes for newsy conversation at each stop. Share news of the parish by chatting with the patients or bringing them their own copies of the parish bulletin or newsletter. This will help those who have dropped out of the mainstream of parish life to feel that they remain members of the parish family. The sick and shut-in parishioners can even be involved in parish activities by praying for the intentions of the local Catholic community. Eucharistic ministers can transform the frustrating futility of the sickroom into a powerful, prayerful extension of any parish effort.

Just as Sts. Aquila and Priscilla "laid down their lives" according to St. Paul's letter to the Corinthians, this openness and love can mean vulnerability for the Eucharistic ministers involved. Listening visitors can fall victim to long-winded, oft-repeated stories or might become privy to old, fermented grudges. Perhaps, the greatest risk is to grow attached to fellow parishioners whose illness ends in death. That particular hurt is the greatest risk of this outreach. A bit of the Eucharistic minister must die each time the footsteps of Sts. Aquila and Priscilla are followed. But this is the price that must be paid in establishing the Church in sickrooms and nursing homes.

# II

# *A Martyr Of The Eucharist*

St. Tarsicius

In the year ad 258, a number of Roman noblemen and senators were attracted to Christianity and joined the Church. Their decision outraged Emperor Valerian who resumed the persecution of the followers of Jesus Christ in the Roman Empire.

Many Christians were thrown into prisons where they were denied any contact with their pastors. One evening, Pope Sixtus II told a congregation gathered in one of the catacombs outside of Rome about the plight of these prisoners who were deprived of any comforts of their faith. Tarsicius, the son of a Roman senator, immediately volunteered to take the Blessed Sacrament to those imprisoned sisters and brothers.

No one is positive of this saintly Eucharistic minister's exact age at this time, but since the sixth century, Catholic tradition has held that St. Tarsicius was a young acolyte. As the youth walked along the famed Appian Way with the Eucharist safely concealed beneath his cloak, he met some of his friends. St. Tarsicius' pals immediately expressed their curiosity in the treasure that he was hiding.

Fearing that they would violate the Blessed Sacrament, St. Tarsicius would not yield to their questions or guessing-games. His acquaintances were enraged. Playful taunts and jostling soon turned to impatient bullying. The young hero of the Eucharist would not give in to their threats. The youths then resorted to mob tactics and began to stone St. Tarsicius, who died rather than surrender the Body of Jesus.

The battered remains of St. Tarsicius, who was later praised by St. Damasus as "the boy martyr of the Holy Eucharist," was buried in the cemetery of St. Callistus.

‡    ‡    ‡

FEW CONTEMPORARY EUCHARISTIC MINISTERS will share St. Tarsicius' call to sacrifice their lives on behalf of the Blessed Sacrament. This apostolate, however, does call for a certain martyrdom and death. At times, the Eucharistic minister is forced to confront death face-to-face; this can be a rare experience in a society such as ours which so often is preoccupied with denying human mortality.

Like St. Tarsicius, Eucharistic ministers will inevitably encounter death while making their rounds. How bravely is such mortality met? Is it possible to honestly talk to someone about death, listen to the patient's fears and then openly share a word of belief and hope? Can death be faced without undue anxiety while holding the hand of a critically ill person who sobs aloud as she waits for the ambulance and yet another dreaded trip to the hospital? Can the routine of the week be followed with the haunting memories of the terminal cancer patient who languishes on his deathbed unable to speak; unable to utter one word? Yes, all this can be endured with faith and a sharing in the death and resurrection of Jesus which is a key element in the Eucharistic minister's outreach to the sick and shut-ins.

Eucharistic ministers can indeed face death and leave with a renewed spirit and life, if this service follows the example given by the boy martyr of the Eucharist, St. Tarsicius, who so intimately shared in these mysteries of Christ. The need to reach out to our infirmed Catholics has to be recognized and met with selflessness and courage. This means that a little of our control, distance and security might have to die along the way.

# III

# The Power Of The Blessed Sacrament

THE POVERTY AND PHYSICAL SUFFERINGS ENDURED by St. Clare of Assisi might seem to make her an ideal patron for those served by Eucharistic ministers. However, her faith and unswerving devotion to the Blessed Sacrament prove her to be a most fitting model for Eucharistic ministers themselves.

Clare was born in 1193, the daughter of an Assisi nobleman, Faverone Offreduccio. The young maiden heard the Lenten homilies of the famed St. Francis of Assisi and was so moved by his eloquent preaching on his beloved Lady Poverty that Clare abandoned all to follow Christ. She "eloped" on Palm Sunday night in 1212 and professed vows to give her life in service of Christ and the poor at Francis' restored chapel, known as the Portiuncula or "Little Portion."

In the coming weeks and months, Clare's vocation was tried by the fire of persecution. Her relatives threatened and cajoled her to return to her fine home. She remained firm to her commitment and eventually she was joined in Religious life by her mother, Ortolana di Fiumi, her sister, Agnes, and other women of the city. The communities founded by Clare began to spring up in other parts of Italy, Germany, France and even in what is now known as Czechoslovakia.

Despite the growth of Clare's spiritual family, she lived a life of humble service and austere penance. During her forty years as abbess of her monastery in Assisi, Clare acted as a "servant of the servants." She waited on tables, cared for the sick Sisters and served as sacristan. Clare was no stranger to illness and she suffered a great deal from a chronic condition especially during the last two years of her life. Yet this did not stop her from spending long hours in prayer before the tabernacle. Even on her sickbed, Clare would spend her time embroidering corporals and other altar cloths.

The true test of St. Clare of Assisi's Eucharistic devotion came in 1244. Emperor Frederick II ravaged Italy and enlisted the assistance of many non-believers who relished the murder and pillage. Eventually, the hordes arrived at the gates of San Damiano. The infirmed Clare ordered her Sisters to carry her to the front wall of the monastery where she raised up the Holy Eucharist enshrined in a monstrance before the raiding party. The raiders were brought to a complete stop. They turned in their tracks and San Damiano was spared.

Nine years later, Clare's final agony began. For seventeen days, she could not eat. Finally, on August 11, 1253, she was lovingly embraced by "Sister Death." Her remains are preserved in Assisi's St. Clare Basilica.

‡    ‡    ‡

JUST AS THE POWER of the Blessed Sacrament is reflected in the life and faith of St. Clare of Assisi, many times Eucharistic ministers are privileged to witness this same miracle in the lives of their patients. Under the guise of Bread, Jesus enters the hearts of these people and dispels their pain and loneliness.

For example, you visit a fellow parishioner who in his prime had been one of the mainstays of the local Catholic community. This man who had been so active and so devoted to the Holy Name Society and the Parents Club now sits and stares vacantly into space. You begin the Communion service with the words of Scripture and you can see that a key word or phrase might momentarily capture this wandering mind. Then as you pray the Our Father with the man's family who is gathered in the kitchen, he joins in the old, familiar words of this prayer from younger, happier times. Just for a moment he is back with those he loves in the present. Then the healing miracle takes place as the Holy Eucharist briefly lifts the veil of confusion.

Then again you have the old couple. Their years of devotion to one another brings new meaning to the term "golden wedding anniversary." You enter their well-kept home where they have lived together all of their adult lives. In a brief conversation, they soon tell you all of their ills and fears, mainly because they have not seen anyone else who listens or who cares. They worry that a minor ache might portend a serious illness; they wonder aloud what happened to the years and where all their old relatives and friends might be; they worry about being forgotten. You share Jesus with them in the Word and the Bread. Like a miracle, after the prayers and communion the old life has returned and they laugh, joke and converse easily.

The Eucharist breaks down barriers of age and isolation. You can see new life surging through arthritic bodies. Listless eyes reflect a new sparkle. The forgotten and depressed seem to sense a new meaning in otherwise empty lives. Often healing tears flow in the wake of these special Communions. A newly arrived nursing home patient knows that he is not going to be forgotten. A chronically ill woman knows that there is hope and peace for her. Anxiety, pain and fear, like the hordes that once threatened San Damiano, fade in the light of the Holy Eucharist.

# IV

## *Longing For The Lord*

### St. Stanislaus Kostka

S TANISLAUS KOSTKA was born at Rostkowo Castle in 1550, the son of Margaret and John Kostka, a powerful Polish senator. The youth grew up with all the advantages available to him in Renaissance Poland, although this wealth and affluence seemed to have little obvious effect on Stanislaus who shunned the court life.

As a teenager, Stanislaus, his older brother Paul and their tutor Dr. John Bilinski traveled to Vienna where Senator Kostka's sons were to continue their education at the Jesuit university. Stanislaus excelled in his classes and grew in his devotion to the Blessed Sacrament. An extension of his love for the Eucharist was his membership in the Confraternity of St. Barbara whose members were assured of the grace of receiving Holy Communion on their deathbeds.

Stanislaus enjoyed his student days in Vienna except for dancing classes and those days when Paul and Bilinski amused themselves by attacking the youth's deep spirituality. The younger Kostka found himself in a very difficult situation after the suppression of the Society of Jesus by Emperor Maximilian II. The Polish brothers and their tutor were forced to leave their rooms at the university and found lodging in the home of a man who was vehemently anti-Catholic.

When a serious illness left Stanislaus Kostka close to death, the saintly young man begged to receive the Blessed Sacrament. However, his landlord refused to allow any priest to enter his house. St. Stanislaus languished on his sickbed longing for the Lord. Then, one night in answer to his most fervent prayers, Mary brought her Son to the infirmed saint and allowed Stanislaus to cradle Jesus in his arms. She promised him a complete recovery and encouraged him to pursue his dream of becoming a Jesuit.

After his health was restored, St. Stanislaus Kostka disguised himself as a poor pilgrim and walked 350 miles to Augsburg, Germany, to seek admission to the Society of Jesus from St. Peter Canisius. The youth took such extreme measures to avoid a confrontation with his father who had vowed to throw the Jesuits out of Poland if they allowed one of his sons to profess vows. Senator Kostka saw such a vocation as a family disgrace!

St. Peter Canisius tested Stanislaus' vocation by various menial and humbling assignments. Convinced of the youth's sincerity, he sent Stanislaus Kostka to the Jesuit novitiate in Rome. The travels and Roman climate drained the frail young man and nine months into his Religious formation, St. Stanislaus Kostka died in Rome on the feast of Our Lady's Assumption. He was eighteen years old.

‡    ‡    ‡

ON A RAINY, Holy Saturday night, an aged widow nervously paced the kitchen floor as she awaited the arrival of her

Eucharsitic minister with whom she would celebrate the ageless Paschal mystery. At long last her wait was over; Christ's courier finally knocked at her door.

After Easter greetings and hugs were exchanged, the Good News of Jesus' resurrection was read; prayers offered and the old woman devotedly welcomed her Lord. Prayers of thanksgiving were not really necessary because tears of joy and gratitude glistened on her furrowed cheeks after this special Easter communion. She smiled as the gloom of a late Spring thunderstorm was dispelled. Indeed, Christ has risen!

This frail immigrant woman captured the finest moment of her fellow countryman and pilgrim: St. Stanislaus Kostka. In her time of infirmity, she too longed for the Lord in the Blessed Sacrament. Through a Eucharistic minister, she was able to embrace her Savior and was revitalized. What greater gifts can any Eucharistic minister receive than to witness such a miracle? How many people linger in pain and loneliness because there is no one available to be the hands and the feet of Christ for them as Eucharistic ministers.

The story of St. Stanislaus Kostka dramatizes the plight of so many sick and aged people throughout the world today. The sufferings of countless people who are confined to their homes or health care institutions are compounded because they lose faith and hope. Eucharistic ministers are needed to care for those who wait, longing for the Lord; longing for the visit of someone who brings the love and the peace of the Eucharist.

St. Stanislaus Kostka focuses our attention on our patients whom we serve and reminds Eucharistic ministers what it is like to suffer alone. He reminds Eucharistic ministers how the sick and aged wait for their comforting presence.

# V

# *The Servant Of The Sick*

## St. Camillus de Lellis

---

Born in the latter part of the sixteenth century, St. Camillus de Lellis led three lives. He knew the glamour of being a playboy and gambler. He enjoyed the adventures of a soldier of fortune. He found his ultimate joy and fulfillment in his commitment to the poor sick. This giant among men, Camillus is said to have stood six feet six inches tall, boasted robust health as a youth and suffered the most annoying, chronic illnesses in his adult years. Now, this well-rounded, Renaissance man is cited by the Church as a most noble "slave of the sick," a title that he willingly adopted during his lifetime.

Known as a rebellious adolescent, Camillus settled down enough to join his father in the fight to save Venice from the Turks. With this taste of military conquest at age seventeen, he was off to a raucous start in life. Camillus spent his days gambling with his life on the battlefields as a mercenary and he spent his nights risking his wages of war at games of chance.

Before his twenty-fifth birthday, he was broke and had to take a job as a laborer constructing a Capuchin monastery.

Camillus experienced a change of heart while engaged in this work and he sought admission to the Capuchin community. His application was rejected because of the horrible sores on his foot and leg that resulted from some disease he contracted during the Battle of Lepanto in the war against the Turks. This and other health problems would bother Camillus throughout the remaining forty years of his life.

When his vocation apparently fell through, Camillus began to minister to the sick of San Giacomo Hospital, Rome, where he had been a patient himself. From this apostolate of a single man evolved a Religious community known as the Servants of the Sick. This Order was established by Father Camillus de Lellis, who had been ordained by the last English bishop in exile, Thomas Goldwell. Their sole mission was to serve the hospitalized, imprisoned and those confined to their homes.

It must have been a sight to see the Father-founder, St. Camillus, roaming the streets of plague-stricken Rome in search of the sick. The former soldier of fortune, dressed in the black cassock and red cross of his Order, went into homes and neighborhoods that others avoided for fear of contracting the dreaded disease. Ever since those days, the Servants of the Sick have followed in the footsteps of St. Camillus. In fact, members of this Order organized the first recorded "military field ambulance" serving on the battlefield of the 1595 war between Hungary and Croatia.

Despite his position as founder and superior, Father Camillus de Lellis always sought out the most repulsive patients to care for and he would often profess how he truly saw Christ in the most wretchedly afflicted. The founder did everything from make beds to hear confessions. He strove to better the lot of those placed in his care.

For many years, St. Camillus not only served his sick but

shared their sufferings by enduring a chronic stomach ailment, loss of appetite and the painful sores on his legs and feet. St. Camillus' earthly life of total commitment to the sick ended with his death in 1614.

‡    ‡    ‡

IN A DIMLY LIT, stuffy sickroom, a once-vital old man struggles to surrender his spirit to the Lord. Unable to eat or even swallow water, he has resigned himself to a slow, painful death. The agonizing weeks dwindle down to the final hours. The death vigil becomes a living nightmare that you want so desperately to forget.

Yet, you come to realize that this is a most holy time and you are graced to share in it. You begin to identify with the feelings of hurt and helplessness which so long ago overcame the Blessed Mother, John and Magdalene at Calvary, when they, like you, looked on the horrible death of a good and just man. You now begin to recognize the face of the suffering Christ in this frail, writhing patient. You are learning the lesson of St. Camillus de Lellis.

St. Camillus reminds us to put aside our own emotions and to look with faith for the face of Jesus in those whom we serve. This great man would meet Jesus in the old woman at the convalescent center, who Sunday after Sunday sits in the same spot staring into oblivion. He would probably see Christ in the man who must search for meaning in his sickness and in the uncertain circumstances which his family must now face. St. Camillus would also feel that he encountered Christ the healer in that ever faithful family which tends to the needs of someone who is chronically ill.

St. Camillus de Lellis, by his example, can heighten the awareness of Eucharistic ministers as to whom they are serving. They serve Him who offered living water and the Bread of Life; they serve Jesus whenever they reach out to the sick.

# VI

## Christian
## In The
## Galleys

ST. PETER CLAVER

THE DISCOVERY OF THE NEW WORLD in 1492 opened doors of fame and fortune to the people of Europe. These opportunities soon gave way to new methods of exploitation and abuse which in turn provided a special ministry for a young Spanish Jesuit seminarian, Peter Claver.

Born in 1581 in Spain's Catalonia region, Peter Claver studied at the University of Barcelona and upon entering the Society of Jesus, he continued his studies at the Jesuit college in Monte Sion at Palma on the island of Majorca. Here, he came under the strong influence of St. Alphonsus Rodriguez, the humble porter of the college. Brother Alphonsus convinced Peter that his call lay in service to the slaves in the New World.

Leaving his homeland forever in 1610, the young Jesuit scholastic embarked for Cartagena, Colombia, the Caribbean port which was the headquarters for the New World's slave trade. An estimated 10,000 people, sold as human cargo, passed through this port each year in the early seventeenth century. Their fate was hopelessly linked to disease, deprivation and hard work in the mines and plantations of the Americas.

In Cartagena, Peter Claver continued his theological studies and served his Jesuit brothers in a variety of menial positions until his ordination in 1615. He then began to collaborate in the ministry of Father Alfonso de Sandoval in spiritual outreach to the slaves who arrived in bondage from their native West Africa.

When a galley ship would arrive at Cartagena and its precious human cargo was herded into cramped pens and sheds, St. Peter Claver and his associates would go to work. St. Peter used to tell his friends, "We must speak to the slaves with our hands before we try to speak to them with our lips." So his first task was to care for the neglected, abused slaves by bringing them medicine, food, brandy, citrus fruits and tobacco. Moving among the diseased, frightened people, the saint would baptize the children and the dying and preach the Good News to the slaves with the help of African interpreters. In 40 years, he received over 300,000 slaves into the Church.

When ships weren't coming in from Africa, St. Peter visited the sick in the general hospital and at the city's leper clinic. He also undertook a special ministry to condemned prisoners. You can imagine that St. Peter Claver was not always held in high esteem by "proper society." Landowners complained that Father Claver's annual missions for his converts on the plantations wasted valuable production time. Fine ladies of the community disliked the Blacks attending Mass in churches around the city. Yet, St. Peter Claver was undaunted despite the criticism.

The years of ministry took their toll on this selfless servant of the slaves. His weakened physical condition made him a susceptible target for an epidemic which swept Cartagena in 1650. He eventually recovered, but his frail body was racked by a palsy that prevented him from celebrating Mass. In his final years, St. Peter Claver was neglected and virtually forgotten, not unlike those whom he served and loved.

Upon his death on September 8, 1654, the Church and state recognized his great contributions. St. Peter Claver was canonized along with his mentor, St. Alphonsus Rodriguez, in 1888. Pope Leo XIII declared St. Peter Claver the universal patron of all missionary efforts among Africans.

‡   ‡   ‡

WHILE EUCHARISTIC MINISTERS frequently find themselves in unpleasant situations, you might find it impossible to even comprehend what St. Peter Claver encountered when he walked aboard the galleys or into the sheds where his beloved flock was confined. Packed together like animals lacking the most rudimentary sanitation, these slaves must have presented a most repulsive picture of humanity. The basic obstacles of language and distrust were further complicated by this miserable atmosphere. St. Peter Claver did not hesitate; he was determined to fulfill his mission.

St. Peter Claver stands as a special model for Eucharistic ministers who find themselves in difficult environments. Certain forms of cancer are accompanied by a foul odor of decaying flesh. While scented candles and strong cologne may somewhat mask the smell, it still pervades the sickroom. The Eucharistic minister may well have to learn to cope with the situation while still taking the time to give this patient extra love and respect. Some people cannot handle the smells and sometimes bedlam noises which they encounter in homes for the aged. The pleading cries and incoherent babbling of some patients who have lost contact with reality are unnerving to say the very least. Some volunteers, who would otherwise gladly visit the hospitalized or the residents of nursing homes, find themselves put off by the distinctly musky odor of nursing homes or the antiseptic smell of hospitals.

Some may find the smells and sounds of modern-day health care facilities to be very repulsive, just as the stench of the slave galleys and the sheds must have assailed St. Peter Claver. Yet, this special man found a certain challenge in this atmosphere. He found grace in these difficult situations and turned the tables in order to see Christ where the rest of the world turned and walked away.

In the slaves, he found a certain liberation in that paradox known to the world as Jesus Christ. Likewise, today's Eucharistic ministers can witness mortality and senseless suffering and in them find their Risen Savior, living forever. Following the footsteps of St. Peter Claver, Eucharistic ministers can find new life in the face of death.

# VII

## *In Partnership With Mary*

VEN. WILLIAM JOSEPH CHAMINADE

---

T HE REIGN OF TERROR known as the French Revolution provided a backdrop of intrigue and suspense for the early ministry of Father William Joseph Chaminade, the saintly priest who founded the Society of Mary. During the dark days of the New Republic when priests and Religious were daily led to the guillotine, Father Chaminade courageously continued his ministry.

Disguised as a farmhand, a filthy ragpicker or a tinker, Father Chaminade would make his way unnoticed through the streets of his native Bordeaux. He would then celebrate secret liturgies in the homes of loyal Catholics. Later, he would make sick-calls, carrying the Blessed Sacrament in a tin pyx which he had fashioned himself. It was not unusual for the young priest to shinny up a drainpipe in order to visit a shut-in without the entire neighborhood and any possible informants knowing about his presence.

Pursued by agents of the French Republic across rooftops and down alleys, seeking refuge beneath barrels and washtubs, the life of Father Chaminade makes exciting reading, but one of his narrowest escapes is of special interest to Eucharistic ministers.

On one occasion, the government agents felt they had finally cornered the elusive "citizen Chaminade," whom they were tailing as the hunted priest made his usual rounds. Knowing that he was followed, Father Chaminade ducked into the home of friends and explained his plight. The head of the household seated the fugitive priest in the midst of the family, who continued their evening prayers.

The agents burst into the house, swearing that they would capture Chaminade this time. They ransacked the dwelling and threatened the owner of the house while Father Chaminade sat calmly in front of them with the rest of the family. After the government men left, the family began to marvel at how Father Chaminade went undetected despite the thorough search. Then the youngest child spoke up, "How could they see Father with the beautiful Lady standing in front of him?"

Mary, the Mother of Jesus, intervened in the life of William Joseph Chaminade many times. As a youth, she healed his badly injured leg. As a Church leader, she revealed to him her plan for the Society of Mary, which would include Sisters, Brothers, Priests and Lay affiliates. And as a minister of the Eucharist, Mary stepped in and helped Father Chaminade at a desperate moment.

Father William Joseph Chaminade died on January 22, 1849 after a lengthy illness and was declared "venerable," an official step toward canonization, in 1973 by Pope Paul VI.

‡    ‡    ‡

ST. LUKE, the physician-evangelist, recounts that Mary was the prototype of all Eucharistic ministers. When her cousin

Elizabeth was pregnant and confined to her home, Mary visited the expectant mother, bringing the future Savior to her home. Joy filled Elizabeth and the life which she carried.

Evidently, the Blessed Mother closely collaborates in the ministry of latter-day Eucharistic ministers as you can see in the vignette about Father Chaminade. Mary can help Eucharistic ministers especially at those times when personal expressions of comfort can seem so inadequate. A nursing home resident cries because she cannot be with her son in a time when he needs her; a woman living alone and battling heart disease cannot comprehend the sudden death of her sister; two brothers barely existing in poverty fear that death will rob them of their sole treasure: each other.

What can anyone say to ease the pain in these cases? Often some sense of peace and comfort come by praying the old familiar words, "Hail Mary, full of grace . . ." Like a good friend or a mother's caress, these prayerful words soothe and comfort. They can bring a sense of peace which helps regain a proper perspective. In sharing the Eucharist with the infirmed, this prayer can set a peaceful tone for the service; actively involve the sick in praying for the intentions of the parish; recognize a special birthday or other milestone in the patient's life.

Mary can also lend a proper perspective to the Eucharistic minister. How much can be learned from this woman who first had the privilege of carrying Jesus in the world? Venerable William Joseph Chaminade learned well from the Blessed Mother. The lessons of this great hero can bear fruit in the work of contemporary Eucharistic ministers.

# VIII

## 'Doctor America' Medical Missioner

### Thomas A. Dooley, M.D.

On January 17, 1927, a contemporary hero for Eucharistic ministers, Thomas Anthony Dooley, first saw the light of day in St. Louis, Missouri. Born the son of a prominent family, the young Dooley had "everything": a dynamic personality, good looks and a solid educational background. He seemed destined to become a social-physician, catering to the aches and ailments of the elite. Contrary to popular speculation, Dr. Tom Dooley was born for greater things.

Tom Dooley's strong commitment to the poor-sick might well be traced to a visit to the Marian shrine at Lourdes when he was a 21-year-old student of French at the Sorbonne. Dooley was appalled by the sufferings of the sick and handicapped who came to this renowned sanctuary in search of healing. Young Dooley returned to the United States and studied at Notre Dame University and St. Louis University Medical School. After graduation, Dr. Dooley served with the United States Navy and assisted in the evacuation of North Vietnam prior to the complete Communist take-over of that section of the southeast Asian country.

These refugees showed symptoms of malnutrition, tuberculosis and malaria. Perhaps, the young Navy doctor was most moved by those victims of Communist torture; they proved their faith by the wounds that they suffered. After his military tour of duty, Dr. Dooley chose to return to Southeast Asia to minister to the poor-sick of Laos, where he found conditions to be extremely primitive. Dr. Dooley was reported to be the only doctor, accredited by Western standards, in a country of two million.

"My work here is not a burden but a privilege," Dr. Dooley once wrote from the hospital that he carved out of the tropical rain forest. In the jungles of Laos, Dr. Dooley not only treated his patients but reached out and bridged cultural differences. He strove to teach good health and hygiene. Working with a small team of volunteers, he was called to service beyond the operating room and did work as painter, plumber and carpenter at his medical mission outpost.

Through all this, Dr. Dooley, who was dubbed "Doctor America" by his native patients, never lost sight of each individual patient. Records may document the thousands who benefited from the mission of Dr. Dooley, but this American physician did not treat numbers or statistics; he treated individuals. This concern for each patient shone through in Dr. Dooley's lecture tours, books and radio tapes which he used to raise funds for his medical missions and to inform the American people of the plight of the southeast Asian.

The medical mission of Tom Dooley grew beyond Laos and became known as MEDICO. In Dr. Dooley's lifetime, he was able to see MEDICO hospitals, clinics and other forms of aid reach out to the people of Laos, Cambodia, Malaysia, Kenya, Haiti, India and South Vietnam. When an infant died of malnutrition in his arms or he treated the victims of poverty, Dr. Dooley seldom despaired. He worked harder to conquer sickness resulting from want and ignorance.

Terminal lung cancer cut short the medical mission of Thomas Anthony Dooley. The diagnosis slowed Dr. Dooley down but was not able to stop him immediately. Dooley served the ill by allowing TV crews to film his surgery and treatment. The award-winning program, "Biography of a Cancer," was broadcast nationally and helped destroy some of the myths surrounding cancer. For over a year, the dying man pushed himself to continue promoting and raising funds for MEDICO. He even made several painful trips back to his beloved Laos.

This great outreach to the poor-sick ended with Dr. Dooley's death on January 18, 1961 in a New York City hospital. He was 34 years old. The vision and charity of Dr. Dooley live on in MEDICO and in those who selflessly serve the poor-sick.

‡        ‡        ‡

IN DR. TOM DOOLEY, the Eucharistic minister can find a modern-day model for selfless dedication to the every need of the infirmed. Dr. Dooley's entire life was consumed by his unwavering devotion to his people. He shows Eucharistic ministers that every means available must be utilized to publicize and meet the needs of the poor sick.

It is very important to note that this young physician transcended the demands of philanthropy. Tom Dooley was more than a concerned citizen; he was a lover of Jesus Christ in the poor-sick. The daily Rosary played an important part in the routine of the isolated jungle hospital where Dr. Dooley served. The young physician would translate the mysteries of Jesus' birth, death and resurrection into his daily healing ministry in Laos. The Rosary charged his work with the presence of Jesus Christ.

Some considered Tom Dooley to be a brash, young "bull-dozer" who was out to make a name for himself. He certainly did generate much publicity, but this was done so that his patients would never be forgotten. This is an important part of the work of today's Eucharistic minister.

After bringing the parish to the hospitalized or shut-in, the Eucharistic minister needs to report back to the parish. A periodic listing of shut-ins in the parish bulletin or newsletter can help the patient maintain a sense of belonging and can keep them from being forgotten during their forced absence. The Eucharistic minister can often learn of the needs of shut-ins, who are often forced to live on fixed incomes. Without violating any confidence, the Eucharistic minister can easily enlist the aid of individuals or organizations in the parish who can meet these needs whether they involve obtaining a walker or hearing aid for a patient or winterizing someone's home. Other parishioners can be involved in improving the shut-ins' quality of life.

With the generosity and creativity of Dr. Tom Dooley, Eucharistic ministers can make a significant outreach in their parishes. How do you gauge the significance of your ministry? Again you take your cue from Dr. Tom Dooley. You never lose sight of the individual. You constantly strive to touch each individual, with his or her particular needs. You act as the hands and feet which enable Jesus in the Blessed Sacrament to meet in a special Communion with this individual.